*Basil in*
*Blunderland*

# Basil in Blunderland

✦⟦○⟧✦

## Cardinal Basil Hume

*with illustrations by*
*Sarah John*

DARTON·LONGMAN+TODD

First published in 1997 by
Darton, Longman and Todd Ltd
1 Spencer Court
140–142 Wandsworth High Street
London SW18 4JJ

Reprinted 1997

ISBN 0–232–52242–1

A catalogue record for this book is available
from the British Library.

Designed by Sandie Boccacci
Phototypeset in 11/15pt Caxton Book by Intype London Ltd
Printed and bound in Great Britain
by BPC Wheatons Ltd, Exeter

# Contents

# *Acknowledgements*

Three people in particular have been closely involved with this book, Heather Craufurd, Sally McAllister and Miles England. I am grateful to them.

I also thank Morag Reeve who, on behalf of Darton, Longman and Todd, took so much trouble in producing this book.

Many young people listened to these stories some twenty years ago. Without them there would have been no book. Thank you for being patient listeners.

*Basil Hume.*

# Prologue

Basil in Blunderland – an odd title for a book, no doubt, and maybe one to surprise. Let me explain. A long time ago – well, nearly twenty years ago – I used to give talks to young people who came from time to time to Archbishop's House. Sometimes sixty or more would come. Many were teenagers. Some were bright, some even brighter. None would claim to be learned. They came for some theology. That gave the whole thing respectability. We used to call those evenings 'theology for the eleven minus'. That, too, may be surprising. In those days there used to be an examination called the 'eleven plus'. If you passed it you went to a school where other clever young people went. If you failed, then you went to a school attended by the less clever but, let me add, equally worthy and good.

Now the talks I gave were entitled 'theology for the eleven minus'. We used the term 'eleven minus' to indicate those who had not passed the 'eleven plus' examination. It was not a clever title, but it served its purpose. We all knew what it meant. If you had passed your 'eleven plus' exam, then you had no place at my talks. You were probably too clever. When we came together we used to discuss important matters about God and ourselves, but in a simple manner. We did not go in for learned footnotes or long words, or thoughts that were too abstract. The talks were simple, solid and, unless I am badly mistaken, interesting too. Exploring God and His world together is interesting, and, indeed, enjoyable too.

Then an important event in my life occurred. On holiday in Scotland, with a family I knew well, I found myself one day being invited by the junior members of the family to play hide-and-seek. There was no problem about that in principle. But on this occasion there was a snag. As a monk I was required to do half an hour's mental prayer each day. That day, when invited to play hide-and-seek, I had not, in fact, meditated. So I had a problem. How does one play hide-and-seek and, at the same time, meditate? Trying to solve that very considerable problem became the subject of my talks to the 'eleven minus'. The hiding places suggested thoughts about the spiritual life.

Then something else happened. The 'eleven plus' examination was abolished, or at least nearly everywhere in the land. It is not for me to judge whether this was sensible or not. Some said it was a mistake, others said it wasn't, but it ruined my title, 'theology for the eleven minus'. No young people now have any idea what 'eleven minus' meant or even the meaning of the 'eleven plus'. The exam simply disappeared and with it the title for this book. That was very annoying, though of no importance to our legislators, or to anyone else for that matter. So I had to change the title. To what, I asked myself? 'Basil in Blunderland' emerged as the right solution. Why?

One day I was thinking about the Caucus-race organised by the Dodo in *Alice in Wonderland*. Sadly, I have an idea that few people read that excellent book these days. Pity. Anyway, let me tell you about that race organised by the Dodo, and how it inspired me.

There had been a great flooding. I read:

> They were indeed a queer-looking party that assembled on the bank – the birds with draggled feathers, the animals with their fur clinging close to them, and all dripping wet, cross, and uncomfortable.

How were they to get dry again? The first solution was to listen to the mouse speaking. But that did not work. The mouse was very boring, as speakers on learned subjects often are.

Then the Dodo had an idea: a Caucus-race. 'What *is* a Caucus-race?' said Alice. 'Why,' said the Dodo, 'the best way to explain it is to do it.' A race-course had to be marked out. Then the race began. There was no 'one, two, three, and away'. Everyone began running when they liked, and left off when it pleased them. Then the Dodo suddenly called out: 'The race is over!' Who has won?, the question was. The Dodo said: '*Everybody* has won, and all must have prizes.'

There is here an important theological point. Life is like a race. It begins and it ends. In the race organised by God, everyone wins. But – and this is quite essential – you have to be involved in the race otherwise you don't get a prize. In God's world everyone is a winner. But you must take part in the race. So don't just listen to people talking or writing about religion. Some do it well, others do not. When they are only concerned with the externals of religion, they make it all sound so boring. Listen again to what the Dodo said about the Caucus-race: 'the best way to explain it is to do it'. So get involved, even if your attempt to do so seems to be a blundering one.

To return to the title, it would have been quite unacceptable to call this book 'Basil in Wonderland'. It would have been far too pretentious. A new title had to be found since 'Theology for the eleven minus' was no longer possible. 'Basil in Blunderland' seemed right. Why? This book is about the spiritual life and in particular is concerned with that aspect of it which is prayer. Now it is a fact that my spiritual life is more a wandering in Blunderland than a resting and relaxing in Wonderland. I would guess that most of us would say the same of ourselves. We have experienced much effort, false starts, wrong decisions, clumsiness. We have no grounds for pride or self-congratulation. That cheers me up rather than depresses. To realise and acknowledge that we are inept and blunderers is healthy. I shall explain.

## About spirituality
It is not right to cultivate inadequacy, but being inadequate, and recognising it, can be, oddly enough, quite comforting. I may blunder into the world of God, but at least I enter into it with a modest opinion of myself. This is called 'humility'. This is a lovely virtue to observe in others, but difficult and painful to acquire for oneself. At least that is my experience. Humility enables us to appear before God in a respectful manner, indeed, on occasions with a healthy (not neurotic) sense of awe and the right kind of fear.

Entering into the world of God is one way of describing spirituality. Spirituality is the soul of religion, its inner dynamism, from which every other Christian action derives its motivation and its energy. Without it religion is empty.

So often religion is seen as something outside us – rules to be obeyed, an ideology to be realised, social action to be taken, an institution with officials and buildings. All of these have a part to play. What matters, however, is that minds and hearts should be involved in that search for God, where the seeking and the finding go hand in hand. It is the process of getting to know God and learning to love Him. It is intimacy with Him that we seek. It is a personal encounter. We try to go beyond every experience of knowledge and love, which we have now, to another experience, which is beyond our grasp but not entirely out of our reach.

The spiritual life is for everybody. If you think it is not for you, then you are wrong, quite wrong. We enter God's world conscious of our inadequacy, of course. We realise, and rightly so, that we are dependent on the guidance of the Holy Spirit, and not on our own meagre resources. We go off in search of God by seeking Him in the created universe and in the Bible where messages from Him are to be found. Our hearts, in yearning for happiness, and for the highest and noblest experience of love, will increasingly long to know Him better. Nearly always desire outstrips knowledge.

## About prayer

The spiritual life and prayer are almost interchangeable words. There is no serious spiritual life without prayer. The problem for most of us is how to get started. Like many worthwhile things it needs a decision to make prayer an integral part of life. It requires, too, a certain amount of organisation. Choose a time of day when you can get away on your own. Don't be over-ambitious. You may only be able to manage five minutes. Don't give up too easily on the pretext that you can't find five minutes, or you can't find a place to be alone. I am not minimising the problems, far from it. But we must not deceive ourselves. Excuses are easy to find.

I should make it clear that the kind of prayer I am speaking about is called 'mental prayer' or 'meditation'. It is different from reciting prayers out of a book or from memory, such as morning and night prayers. These, incidentally, are also quite essential. I have in mind time spent alone with God, trying to raise mind and heart up to Him.

Now there are many teachers of the spiritual life today. The desire for spirituality and the need for a life of prayer are perhaps among the most significant and important aspects of life in the Church today. And it is noteworthy that many of these teachers are women.

I return to the question of mental prayer. We need starting points. Let me tell you about mine. I have several. First, I have always been influenced by what St Paul wrote in his letter to the Romans. This is the text:

> For what can be known about God is plain to them, because God has shown it to them. Ever since the creation of the world his invisible nature, namely, his eternal power and deity, has been clearly perceived in the things that have been made.
>
> (Romans 1, 19–20)

I understood from this that there are many hints in the created universe of what God may be like. Such hints are no doubt very different from the reality, but nonetheless are helpful. For instance, we have been told that we are made in the image and likeness of God. It means that what we see in others may give us some idea of what God is like. Thus beauty in people, goodness and nobility may lead us – should lead us – to think of God. The same line of argument applies to all that strikes us as true and good. There are important hints in each of these. We do well to reflect on beauty, goodness and truth and try to relate them to God.

You see a beautiful person? How much more beautiful is God. Beauty in Him may well be different, and indeed it is. But a beautiful person or object points to the presence of a similar value in Him. God is responsible for all beauty. The work of art tells us something about the artist.

You seek truth? As you do so, you are exploring the mind of God, seeing persons and things as He sees them.

You are drawn to what is good, and therefore lovable? Then in some manner you are drawn to Him who is the cause of the good in persons and things. The goodness that attracts reflects the goodness and lovableness which God is. God is lovable, the most lovable of all. A person in love is well placed at that moment to glimpse the meaning of the word 'love' as used of God.

This, I recognise, is a learned point. Do not be put off. Think about it.

A second starting point is this. It is to think about Jesus Christ and to listen to His words. You will remember how one day the apostle Philip said to Jesus: 'Show us the Father and we shall be satisfied' (John 14,8). Jesus answered: 'Philip, you have been with me all this time, have you not realised that he who sees me sees the Father?' (John 14,9). In other words, in Our Lord's words, actions, and attitudes we learn in a human way truths about God Himself. Jesus Christ is both God and man. Let me give you an example: some words of Our Lord, recorded by St Matthew, can be very consoling to those who, for one reason or another, are in difficulties or in pain. 'Come to me, all who labour and are heavy laden, and I will give you rest' (Matthew 11,28). These words, like all Christ's words, are personal to each one of us, and always relevant. The cultural context may be different, but the truths taught are contemporary in every age. Read such words as if Our Lord Himself were whispering them into your ear. In fact, He is doing so. As you think about them ('ruminate' might be a good word in this context) they may, if God so wills it, begin to warm your heart. When such words affect you, giving light to the mind and warmth to the heart, it is because the Holy Spirit is at work within you.

A third starting point is to repeat slowly and, of course, prayerfully a phrase from the Gospel. For example, such phrases as 'Jesus be merciful to me a sinner', or 'Lord, thou knowest all things, thou knowest that I love you', or 'Lord, I believe, help Thou my unbelief' or 'Into Thy hands, Lord, I commend my spirit'. This last is a powerful prayer. They are the words prayed by Our Lord on the Cross. They express, or try to, our total abandonment to God's will. With these words we accept the trials of life, and then, as we get older, death itself. So, your thoughts should be directed to the person you are addressing. The words lead you to think about the person. Our Lord. Then the words may become secondary, and you know – perhaps only in a confused way – that He is present with you.

A fourth way of praying is to recite silently and very slowly, a well-known prayer like the Our Father or one of the 150 psalms. Jesus Christ gave us the Our Father Himself so it has a privileged place in the prayer of the Church. The psalms are particularly wonderful prayers. Our Lord prayed them in His lifetime; the Church, the Body of Christ, does so all over the world and in every age. The Jewish community prays the psalms. When we do so we are linked to our Jewish roots, and very much in communion with the whole Judaic tradition. As you read or recite, try to go beyond the words to the thoughts they are expressing, and then direct the thoughts to the Person you are seeking to address. There may come a moment when you do not wish to continue reading. You just want to dwell and rest on a word or phrase that speaks powerfully to you at that moment. Maybe you will sense the presence of Him whom your heart is seeking. I say 'maybe', for I do not know whether this can happen often or very rarely.

Lastly, I would like to remind you of the 'prayer of incompetence'. Sometimes our minds are possessed by a great worry or agony. We cannot, try as we will, escape from it. It is there, and there it remains. At other times we may be mourning a loved one. The sense of grief and sorrow drives out every other thought. The loss just hurts. Then there will be occasions when physical pain clouds the mind. It seems to mock at fine thoughts. The way to pray this 'prayer of incompetence' is just to be in the presence of God, though this presence will be far from apparent. Just 'be' with the pain, and perhaps murmur, 'Lord, let this chalice depart from me . . . . but not my will but thine be done'. Or kiss the wounds of Christ on a crucifix. If you are sick in bed make sure you have a crucifix or a rosary under the pillow. Kissing those wounds is excellent prayer.

Each of these starting points may well lead to silence. Just to be silent with an awareness of God is a high point of the prayer I have been describing. For many of us, we get no further than the starting points. The golden moment of silence eludes us. Do not worry. Prayer is trying to raise mind and heart to God. If the golden moment occurs, it is His gift. If it does not, your prayer is still most pleasing to God. In fact, the starting point may be the point of arrival. A lifetime of starting once again every day makes us different, more Christ-like. Others notice. We don't. Our consolation and joy may not come during the daily effort to raise mind and heart to God. It may happen differently. As the Dodo said, 'the best way to explain it is to do it'.

## About the game

We are now ready to start the game of hide-and-seek. Readers may be a little baffled about how it worked. But read on. It will become clear. Anyway, I trust so. Like prayer, 'the best way to explain it is to do it'. One aspect of the game troubled me for a moment. This book records the thoughts and reflections prompted by the hiding place. Quite often I would think about the principles of the spiritual life in general rather than about God and His world. I should have been praying, but thoughts about the spiritual life barged their way into my attempts to pray. It is so often so. It is better to pray than to speak about it. Obvious. Maybe I would have done better to have got down on my knees and prayed than to have produced a book like this.

Then another anxiety entered my head. Rereading what I have written in this book seemed to be much more 'eleven plus' than 'eleven minus'. The scruple went away quickly when I recalled that yesterday's 'eleven minus' group are now much older, wiser and more experienced. And so am I. So you are invited to join the members of that lovely group who listened to earlier versions of these talks. They were patient and understanding. I trust that you, the reader, will be also.

Now to the game. Kate and Barney are getting impatient.

# The Larder

⊷⟹⟸⊶

We had to decide who was going off to hide first. The choice was Barney. Kate and I turned round and faced the wall and started to count up to twenty, very slowly, of course. Barney shot off as quickly as he could. I would like to remind you that when playing hide-and-seek, once you have found the person then you let out a great shout of triumph. That is the end of that round. But the game we were playing was slightly different. Once one of us had found the person hiding, the two of us would stay together until the third had succeeded in discovering us. It is a special kind of hide-and-seek.

I found Barney first. He was in a room which is generally next to the kitchen. It is a very important room. It is called the larder. Larders used to be even more important when there weren't any of those modern things like fridges and freezers. How on earth did we manage without a fridge? Sometimes there was a kind of detached extension to the larder. This was often in the back-yard. It had a funny door with lots of holes in it so that air could get in and the cat could not. But you couldn't hide here. The entrance was too small. But this is all slightly by the way. The larder proper was where you had sacks of potatoes on the floor and dishes of yesterday's food on the shelves. Its entry was from the kitchen. Barney was hiding in the larder. Kate had gone off in a different direction, so I had plenty of time to continue my meditation. I started to think about the larder. I remembered something that I was told when I was a very small boy. This is the story.

In a larder there was a stack of apples. Nobody knew exactly how many. A small boy wanted an apple. He had been told by some grown-up that he must not take things from the larder without permission. Taking things without permission that belong to other people was called 'stealing'. But, as I have said, nobody knew how many apples there were and, in any case, the small boy was all alone in the larder. Why not take one? Nobody would know. It just seemed common sense. He was hungry and wanted an apple. Why should he not have one? Nobody would see him. Was that true? Nobody? One person would. That was God. He sees everything you do, and then punishes you for the wrongdoing, so I was told.

It took me many, many years to recover from that story. Deep in my subconscious was the idea of God as somebody who was always watching us just to see if we were doing anything wrong. He was an authority figure, like a teacher or a policeman or even a bishop.

Now, many years later I have an idea that God would have said to the small boy, 'Take two'. I must explain that God never encourages us to steal. I have to make this rather obvious and ponderous statement because someone – no doubt learned and very good – once wrote to me to explain that God doesn't want us to steal. Of course not. So please do not go round to your neighbourhood greengrocer and take two apples!

The point of my story is to explain that God is not the kind of person who is watching you all the time to catch you out. He is on our side unless we walk away from Him deliberately. If our idea of God is of a stern authority figure, then we shall always be a little bit twisted. Fear will be dominant in our relationship with God. We have to think of Him, not as an authority figure, but as a loving father.

One day I told this story on radio. It later appeared in a parish magazine. A lady wrote to me and said: 'I read your story about the larder. It reminded me of something told to me by an aunt.' She went on to describe how in the aunt's house there was one of those funny old notices in flowery writing. It was a passage from scripture. The text was: 'Thou God seest me'. But the lady said, 'Yes, God is always watching you. Because He loves you so much He cannot take His eyes off you.'

That is a wonderful thought. God can't take His eyes off me.

Wherever I am and whatever I am doing, He keeps looking at me, not to catch me out, but from love. As lovers look for each other and then gaze at each other, so it is with God.

In a quiet moment we may just let our thoughts dwell on the simple truth that God cannot take His eyes off us because He loves us so much. There is encouragement enough to make us want to find out more about God, what He is like, what we mean to Him.

Realising that God loves us is a transforming experience. It marks a change from a religion based in the main on fear. Fear is common. It is also intolerable. There are those who flee from fear simply because they cannot live with it as a burden to be carried. There is, of course, a fear that is healthy. We do not wish to displease God; we do not want to yield to temptation; we feel guilty when we have sinned seriously or deliberately and we are fearful of the consequences. But our permanent state of mind should be one of joy, knowing that God loves us dearly and is rich in mercy and understanding.

Eventually Kate arrived. I had to bring my meditation to a close. I was now prepared for the next round of hide-and-seek. I felt so much happier now because once again I had reflected on the great love which God has for me. And I decided I didn't want to do anything wrong because I didn't want to displease One who loved me so much and trusted me so greatly. Who goes off to hide now?

# The Clock

It was Kate's turn to hide, so Barney and I started to count, facing the wall, of course. Kate went halfway up the stairs where there was a grandfather clock. She had to squeeze in behind it. Thank goodness, Kate is pretty thin. Barney and I set off to look for her. Barney was slightly ahead of me. He shot straight past the clock without realising that Kate was behind it. This was quite surprising, because as I followed him up the stairs, I spotted Kate's elbow sticking out from behind the clock!

There was no way that I could squeeze in behind her, so I decided to wander off and flop into a chair in the first room I could find. This was quite an advantage because I was able to continue my meditation in a comfortable armchair on my own.

I began to think about the clock. It was old and rather beautiful. Unlike many other grandfather clocks that I have met, this one actually worked. I began to reflect: every time the big hand moved round I was that much older and – a rather sombre thought – that much closer to death. But my meditation on death ceased there. It would have been depressing to go on that way. I was in no mood to be depressed. Yes, I know it is a good thing to meditate on death, but no, not today.

As I was thinking about the clock I recalled a phrase which came from a great spiritual writer. He spoke about 'the sacrament of the present moment'. Now you know that a sacrament is an event where God enters into our lives. It is an outward sign of an inner grace (either a share in God's own life or a special help being given to us). Christ meets us in the sacraments, especially in the Eucharist. There are only seven sacraments, so what is this 'sacrament of the present moment'? Is there an eighth sacrament?

Before thinking further about this I began to think about 'time', or rather about the idea of the present moment. (If you dislike complicated thoughts about 'time', leave out the next paragraph, but don't fail to read the one after.) I say to myself, 'now', and no sooner have I said it than it has already passed. I cannot hang on to 'now'. It's gone. Another 'now' has taken its place. Life is a succession of 'nows'. You cannot prevent the clock from showing us how time marches on. I remember once looking at a clock at the moment it stopped. I said 'now', and there wasn't another one. I realised that eternity is like a 'now' which goes on and on. The earthly clock stops and we are riveted for ever in the presence of God. Sometimes as we go through life there are moments to which we just want to hang on. It may be a moment of total happiness, one that is completely satisfying or very thrilling. We just want time to stop. That tells me something about what it must be like in heaven. In heaven there is a 'now' of total happiness when we are with God. The vision of God is so fulfilling and totally satisfying. It is an ever-present 'now' of ecstatic love when we are one with the most lovable.

Where, then, does 'the sacrament of the present moment' come in? A sacrament, as I have already said, is an event where Christ meets us and we meet Him. When you come to think of it the present moment can be a meeting point between God and us. It is only 'now', in the present moment, that we meet Him, here and now. Some people spend a lot of time looking back on their lives, others spend time daydreaming about the future, but the important moment is 'now'. In any present moment we can meet God. At any moment we can just think about God and send a quick message up to Him. It may be a fleeting thought or a word spoken. For instance, I can just say 'I am trying to love you', or 'please help me', or 'I am sorry about this or that'. The present moment is always precious. Like a sacrament it is a meeting point between God and ourselves.

I stayed sitting in a chair for a long time because Barney was wandering all over the house quite unable to find Kate. The clock continued to go round, time was passing, and, unless Barney turned up pretty soon, there would not be time to play any further rounds of hide-and-seek, nor for me to continue with my meditation.

Basil in Blunderland

Kate and I were just a little irritated when Barney finally appeared. 'Oh,' said Barney, when eventually he turned up. 'My watch had stopped, and I didn't know the correct time.' 'That is no excuse, Barney,' I said, in no way hiding my irritation. The present moment, I recalled, is like a sacrament, when I can meet God. This time, however, I remembered to raise my mind and heart to God. I said a quick prayer. 'Sorry, Lord, for being annoyed with Barney. Next time I'll be patient. Promise.' When you are irritated count ten before you speak, I was told. I never do, and always regret it afterwards.

# The Telephone

At the end of a corridor and just around the corner was the telephone. It was not easy to find. It was, moreover, always very cold in that part of the house. I think this was done to make it difficult for visitors to make telephone calls. Barney went and hid there. When I found him I went into a nearby bedroom, flopped into a chair and continued my meditation.

I began to think of an aunt of mine – I call her Auntie B – who was very old and extremely deaf. Telephoning her was, on the whole, an unrewarding experience. She could not hear what I was saying. She disliked telephones anyway. She had very little to say. Why, then, did I telephone her? Simply because it was good to know that she was there, and to realise that she was pleased that I had taken the trouble to call her.

Many of us have this kind of experience when we pray. It is like telephoning somebody who appears to be deaf and apparently has nothing to say to us. But then God does not have ears like us. Nor does He have a voice like ours. So what is the point of phoning Him, that is praying to Him? Sometimes I say to myself that God is like Auntie B, bad on the telephone. Nonetheless when I begin to speak to Him in prayer I sense that He is pleased that I am doing so. He is pleased that I am paying attention to Him. When I pray I know that He is there listening to what I have to say. But does He answer when I make my requests? Has He heard me? I realised long ago that I had to have faith and patience that, in fact, God answers our prayers in His way and not in ours. Now He knows what is good for us and what is harmful. In fact, He has only one desire for us. It is that we should get closer to Him and eventually be given the gift of everlasting life with Him. Whatever helps that, we shall receive, whatever does not lead to that, we shall not. Nonetheless every prayer we say draws us closer to Him.

One of the advantages of speaking, or better trying to speak, with Auntie B was that it jolted her memory to send me every year at Christmas a box of chocolates. I think I am being honest enough to say that I did not just telephone her in the course of the year in order to get my Christmas present. In fact, I had not asked for them. She sent them because she thought that I was getting too thin and I needed something to make me fatter. So sometimes God sends us a gift of some kind long after we have made our prayer of petition. Often it is something quite unexpected like a new understanding of what He is like or a special help in a time of crisis. In any case every prayer I speak is pleasing to Him. I think I can say that when I spoke on the phone to Auntie B, I did it to please her. I know that when I pray to God it pleases Him.

Suddenly the telephone, which was at the end of the corridor but around the corner, began to ring. Neither Barney nor I knew what we should do. When I picked up the receiver I just heard the sound of heavy breathing, like a great sigh. That can be quite a sinister sound and frightening. I learned later

that this was a sigh from somebody who could not speak properly, but just wanted to be in touch with the owner of the house. Then I began to think about that sigh. The Holy Spirit is a 'sigh' of love coming from the Father and the Son. St John tells us that. Our Lord breathed on the Apostles and in that manner gave them the Holy Spirit. When we pray to God the Father, He utters an inaudible sigh, a gentle breathing like a friendly breeze. It is the Holy Spirit entering into our minds and hearts.

# The Television

It was Kate's turn to hide next and she made her way into a small room at the end of a long corridor. The television set was there. It was quite a good idea to hide there because she could watch television. The two of us who were seeking her would think that somebody else was occupying that room. When, eventually, I found her, I went and found a quiet place nearby to continue with my reflections.

I remember somebody watching television with me. He had that maddening habit of what I believe is called 'surfing'. I think this means flicking from one station to another. He never seemed to settle on any one of them. I could not but reflect how the human mind can be rather like someone going from one programme to another. A succession of thoughts and images go through my head exactly as I have seen on the television set. This is very trying when it comes to praying. Images and thoughts too often crowd into my head when I find it so difficult to think just about God. We call these distractions.

While I was making these reflections I suddenly decided to go into the television room and join Kate. She was not really 'surfing' but she did get bored with one programme quite quickly. She found nothing to hold her attention. I sat next to

her and gazed at the screen. Then something quite helpful dawned on me. Quite often I go to pray and find it difficult to concentrate on God. In my head there is a succession of thoughts and images, and most are quite irreligious. It occurred to me that I should invite God to come and sit by my side. Then I would say to Him, 'all these thoughts and images which are rushing through my mind, I ask you to watch them with me'. And so these images and thoughts become my prayer because I have asked Him to watch them with me. It doesn't always make coping with distractions any easier. I just try to say a quick word to God: 'help me to bring you into my confused thoughts'. So I reflect: that tricky problem I must face tomorrow, or next Saturday's football results (I sometimes score a really good goal – I am ashamed about that, I mean about the distraction, not the goal – it was quite brilliant!), or the birthday present I have forgotten to buy. 'Bring them to God', I say to myself. If I learn to take my distraction to God, then I get into the habit of bringing God into my daily life.

Experience has shown me that reflective praying – which we call meditation or mental prayer – is much better done early in the morning. As the day's affairs gather momentum, so our minds become increasingly cluttered – at least for most of us. Others prefer to pray in the evening after the day's work. Much depends on our temperaments as to which we find the easier. We must never use 'distractions' as an excuse not to pray. People do. 'Prayer isn't for me,' they say. Wrong. Prayer is for everyone. So remember once again that prayer is trying to raise our minds and hearts to God. Sometimes the 'trying' has to be done through what seems to be a real battle to concentrate on God. Never mind. Just keep trying. That pleases God, and one day you will discover peace in his presence, a reward, I like to think, for our perseverance.

Distractions are, then, part of the experience of praying. We can't escape altogether from them.

'So, Lord, I go on now trying to fix my thoughts on You. I find that I cannot get out of my head an anxiety which has been bothering me these last few days. Lord, may I share it with You?' I just sit quietly, and the persons I am worried about appear one by one in my mind. As I see each one I offer them to God to give them His care – and, I ask Him to resolve my anxiety. And, I would like to be freed from distractions just for a little time – well, till the next one comes along.

There are times when we are in the grip of a great pain. We have lost one we loved much. There has been a disaster in the family or one that threatens. We have been cruelly treated by others, accused unjustly, ridiculed. Thoughts about God do not come. Words do not help. On these occasions just kneel or sit, and pray 'not my will be done, Lord, but yours'. Just remain agonising, knowing that the Gethsemane experience can lead – perhaps a long way ahead – to a Mount Tabor one. It was on Mount Tabor that Christ was transfigured. Peter said on that occasion: 'It is good, Lord, for us to be here.' It is always a privilege to join Christ in His agony in the Garden. But it does hurt.

# The Stairs

As we were deciding whose turn it was to hide next, we passed the main staircase. I noticed something very interesting. At the top of the stairs was the gentleman who owned the house. I have not introduced him yet because he was not part of our game of hide-and-seek. He was around in the house to make sure, I think, that we did not break things, or fall down the stairs or generally cause chaos. His was a very discreet presence. In any case he had to look after Simon. Simon was only two years old.

This is what happened. Simon's father was standing at the top of the stairs. Simon himself was trying to get up on to the first step. This two-year-old was making every effort to get up that first step. Simon is not bad on the flat but he does not seem to have mastered the technique of going up and down stairs. I watched him as he put his foot on the first step and then, predictably, he fell backwards. And, equally pre-dictably, Simon let out a terrific howl. He soon calmed down and he continued trying to get up that first step. Every effort turned out to be a failure. Then the obvious thing happened. His father came down the stairs, picked Simon up and carried him to the top.

Later in the evening I began to reflect. What struck me was the fact that Simon's father, having carried him up the stairs, hugged him, gave him a kiss and then put him back at the bottom of the stairs again. He told Simon to go on trying to get up that first step. If he did not make the effort he would never succeed.

This turned out to be, at least for me, a kind of parable of the way it is in the spiritual life. We do our best to pray. It is like putting a foot on the bottom step and failing, or seemingly so, to get up on to it. We try and try again and go on failing. We have various options, as indeed Simon had. He could just sit there and howl, or he could just decide there was no future in trying to get upstairs, so he would simply walk away and go into another room. In other words he would just give up. It was because his father saw him trying that he was prepared to come down and give Simon the help which he needed. Simon could not get up to the top of the stairs, unless his father came down to pick him up. So it is with us.

We go on trying to pray and we do not succeed. Now we could just sit down and complain bitterly that prayer is not for us, or we could just walk away and do something else. But the right thing is to keep on trying. Then our heavenly Father, seeing us trying and delighting in watching us, will come down, pick us up and take us to the top of the stairs. I am referring to those few but golden moments when in prayer we just feel at ease in the presence of God. Such moments can be very rare. Most of the time we just have to go on trying to raise our minds and hearts to God. But then, after God has carried us to the top, and embraced us, we find we have to start all over again. Our part is to try to raise our minds and hearts to God. If there are moments when we seem to be in His presence, that is because He came and carried us up to the top of the stairs. It is His gift. And when we go on trying to pray we can live on in the memory of that golden moment. For some of us this sense of God's presence is very rare. For others, it never seems to happen at all. But one thing is certain, we must just go on trying. This can be quite tedious. But it is helpful to bear in mind that we have our part to play in the business of praying, and God has His. Ours is to keep going, learning all the time that praying is something we do for God's sake – to give Him honour and glory – and not for ours. Whatever we get out of it is His gift. Maybe we are left to go on persevering without reward in order to learn that we must wait on God to reward us if and when He chooses.

# Under the Piano

Barney and Kate decided that I should hide next. So I went off and hid under the piano. I was just a little bit anxious about this because I was not too certain that my arthritic hips would fold up all that easily. It might be thought that there was nothing particularly subtle about going under the piano because it is extremely difficult to hide under a piano and not be seen. Not so in this case. This piano was ancient. The people in the house were hoping to sell it. They did not want it to get too tatty on top so there was a cloth draped over it hanging down to the floor. Then all kinds of things were put on top of the piano: photographs, trinkets given as Christmas presents and, I noticed, a flowerpot which seemed to have got a little too near the edge of the piano for comfort.

There was an unwritten rule that one should not hide under the piano just in case it got damaged further, and its value on the market would be less. I felt a little bit deceitful in breaking that unwritten rule. It gave me, however, a lot of time to meditate.

I began to think about the piano. My mind travelled to a parish church, where the harmonium was not in very good shape and neither was the lady who played it. The harmonium was out of tune and the player out of sorts. The result was

a very grim noise, as you can well imagine. The choir was on bad form too. I noticed that there was, as so often happens, one person with a very loud voice, one that was not particularly melodious. I continued to reflect on the liturgy as celebrated in that particular church. The harmonium was out of tune, the choir dreadful and the priest . . . well, Father could not sing either. Then I asked myself in my meditation, how on earth could the sound from that harmonium, the lack of skill of the player, the flat and dull voice of the priest and that choir, be in any way pleasing to God.

Then I remembered how often some people complain about the liturgy in their parish. They use words like 'ghastly' and 'boring'. So is bad liturgy of this kind displeasing to God? I then understood that God never looks for success but is always pleased when we try to do our best. Now it is quite obvious that, when we come to the worship and praise of God, we must spare no trouble in preparing the liturgy and making the music and singing as beautiful as possible. We can never take too much trouble to get it right. But many of us are not able to make the music and the singing good. Often we have to put up with musical instruments that are either untuned or unpleasing to the ear. God, as I say, looks at the effort we make and is pleased with that. I think – and I hope that I am not deceiving myself – that God prefers humble failures to proud achievers.

It would be lovely if the harmonium were played with the skill of a cathedral organist, or if the singing sounded like a choir of professionals, wonderful if the priest had a melodious voice, so that had he not been a priest he would have been an opera singer. It would help if the church were not so draughty and the benches not so uncomfortable. What a joy it would be if the whole congregation could sing with skill and gusto, instinctively breaking into four parts. In most parishes it is not like that, or seldom is.

I continued my meditation, thinking of a passage from C.S. Lewis in his book entitled *Letters to Malcolm*. This is what he wrote:

> It is along these lines that I find it easiest to understand the Christian doctrine that Heaven is a state where angels now and men hereafter are perpetually employed in praising God. This does not mean, as it can so dismally suggest, that it is like being in church. For our services, both in their conduct and in our power to participate, are merely attempts at worship, never fully successful, often 99.9% failures, often total failures. We are not riders but pupils in the riding school. For most of us the falls and the bruises, the aching muscles and the severity of the exercise far outweigh those moments in which we were, to our astonishment, actually galloping without terror or disaster. At present we are merely, as Donne says, tuning our instruments. The tuning of the orchestra can be delightful but only to those who in some measure, however little, anticipate the symphony. The Jewish sacrifices and even our most sacred rites as they occur in human experience are, like the tuning, promise not performance. Hence, like the tuning, they have in them much duty and little delight or none. But the duty exists for the delight. When we

carry out our religious duties we are like people digging channels in a waterless land, in order that when at last the water comes it might find them ready, I mean for the most part. There are happy moments, even now, when a trickle creeps along the dry beds, and happy souls to whom this happens often.

So we should think of our parish liturgy as 'the tuning of the instruments' preparing for the perfect song of praise when we shall be in the very presence of God and see him face to face. It will be a song of praise in tune, melodious and just a delight to be involved. No, I won't wince any more, when the music jars and the hymns seem to me to be banal. Anyway, I don't sing in tune, so why should I be so critical of others. Forgive me, Lord.

Yes, it will often be 'ghastly' and 'boring', but then we must ask ourselves a question. Do we go to Mass in our parish church in order to be entertained or in some way to be fulfilled? Or do we go because it is important to be there, and to contribute our best to the praising and worship of God, and for His sake and not ours? 'Boring' is not a word that should enter into the vocabulary of prayer.

At that point Barney had worked out that I was under the piano. He rushed in, banged into the piano and the flowerpot fell on to the ground. I knew it would. The noise it made told Kate where we were. Now we had to go off and own up to being responsible for the breaking of the flowerpot. Perhaps I was wrong to hide where I knew I shouldn't be. Oh dear, I have been rightly punished.

# The Window

Barney now hid behind the curtain in the drawing room. I got behind another curtain in the same room once I had found him. Curtains in old houses can be very musty. What I particularly dislike is the way they harbour cigar smoke. Well, there was no alternative to staring out of the window, and getting on with my attempts at meditation.

I got very little encouragement from looking out of the window. It was foggy outside, and as bad a fog as you would get anywhere. It would have been helpful had there been a lovely view, or a pleasant garden to look at. But fog has nothing to say to me. It won't help my prayer. No, of course, I am wrong. Fog has in fact a good deal to say to me. 'Can't you understand?' I said to myself. Think about that fog in your head. Then I remembered those days when thinking about God was more or less impossible. The words I used seemed to have no meaning; thoughts about God or about the truths of the Gospel seemed quite dead. The fog outside was damp and very cold; my mind and heart were cold. But I shall keep going, either saying the words or trying to think about God. I shall not walk away from the window because there is only fog to look at. I won't walk away from prayer even if today thoughts and words are quite meaningless.

So I just went on gazing out of the window, irritated by the smell of the curtains, not anxious to open the window even a little. Then suddenly the fog lifted. It began to waft away. I now saw what the fog had hidden, a lovely view of the garden. The colours of the flowers seemed to dance before my eyes, and their beauty sent messages to my mind to express delight in what I saw. My mood changed. Indeed, I no longer bothered about the smell of the curtains for I had opened the window and rejoiced in the scent of the flowers and that most exquisite of all smells, the smell of cut grass. If I hadn't continued to look out of the window, I would have missed that magic moment.

It is often thus in prayer. As I have said already, so often words and thoughts are quite hopeless, for there is fog in my mind, or at least there seems to be. But stick at it, say the words, try to think. Don't walk away. Suddenly the fog will lift. The words or the thoughts will begin to send their messages to mind and heart. Dry and cold before, they now come to life. In the fog I said 'Lord, I want to love you', and it seemed remote and untrue. But I kept at it. The fog lifted, and when I repeated that prayer, it came to life. I really wanted to say it.

I went on gazing out of the window, but, alas, the fog came down again, and hid the garden from my view. I closed the window. The curtains seemed even more musty than before. The words 'Lord, I want to love you' now ceased to inspire me. It is like that in the spiritual life – moments of delight, followed by dryness and coldness. But never walk away. Go on praying, and wait for the fog to lift again or even one day to go away altogether.

Kate had by now arrived. She said: 'Let's go out into the garden, and play there.' 'Haven't you seen the fog?' I asked. She hadn't. So I said, 'We shall go outside later.'

I was disappointed not to be able to go outside. Sad, too, that all that was beautiful in the garden was hidden from my view by the fog. Beauty in all its forms can play a vital part in helping me to raise mind and heart to God. Beauty is a message from God. It says to me: if this flower is beautiful or that view, if this piece of music is beautiful, or that lovely building, what must God be like? He is the author of all beauty. Beauty is a hint of the way beauty is in Him. Beauty, seen or heard, carries us into His presence. We can pray with our eyes, and our ears, without words, just admiration. Admiration leads to praise. And, by the way, to go on praising God, when the fog has come once more into our minds, is excellent prayer. It may not be much fun, but it is a sign of our generosity. We sing the praises of God for His sake, not for ours. He doesn't need our prayer, I hear you say. I wouldn't be too sure of that. In any case, if the fog clouds our minds, memories of light from the past are reason enough for us to carry on with our songs of praise.

# The Fire

Barney went off and hid under a sofa. In fact it was Kate's turn, but Barney thought it was his. Never mind. Life is rarely fair. Barney had one of his feet sticking out, which really wasn't very clever of him. I told him to hide properly. Meanwhile I sat down on the sofa. Then Kate arrived. She immediately spotted Barney's foot, which somehow had wandered out again from beneath the sofa. The three of us decided we needed a rest. The game was getting very tense. The sofa was the obvious place to sit. It was an old broken-down sofa, not very comfortable, because some of the springs

had ceased doing a respectable job. The sofa was in front of a fire. Barney and Kate began to chat to each other and this suited me. I was able to get on with meditating – well, up to a point since chattering between two people nearby makes prayer difficult. We need silence. At least I do.

I must explain that this was an old-fashioned house so there were no electric fires or gas fires which dry up the atmosphere. Indeed there weren't even any radiators. But there were real fires with real flames and lots of wood to be burnt, stacked up in the fireplace.

I began to think about the fire. This one was very warm and it gave out a lot of heat. That is quite surprising because in most old houses the heat goes up the chimney. But this fire was not just warm, it was also friendly. Proper fires can be friendly. Electric fires, gas fires and radiators are useful, of course, but who wants to sit and look at any of these? Imagine sitting in front of a radiator for an hour. A fire mesmerises me as I sit and watch the flames. Watch the flames, and they seem to dance. They are never quite still. A warm and friendly fire is an image of God. Anyway it makes me think of God. The fire is not only friendly, but it is also very active. It is a good image of God, who is quite still, but immensely active. In fact, I find the flame of a candle to be an even better image. When you look at it the flame seems to stand still (unless there is a draught, which is highly likely in an old house) but the chemical reaction which is going on all the time causes the flame to be very active. God never changes, is always quite still, but He is always very active, and creative all the time.

## The Fire

As I have said, the fire is warm and friendly and that is why it makes me think about God. Incidentally, I am just wondering whether you have got another thought in your mind. When we talk about fire, we think about hell-fire. There must be a very interesting connection between the fire that gives warmth and the fire that destroys. But that is a learned point, and I don't want to begin to deal with it in this book.

There are two fires in the Bible. You can read about one of them in the Old Testament. It is the story of Moses discovering a burning bush. The bush burns, but it is not destroyed. Moses hears the voice of God saying 'I am who I am' or, as some people would say, 'I am what I am'. The burning bush reveals the presence of God. The words 'I am what I am' also mean that God is a loving person. He says, 'I am warm and friendly'. The other fire in the Bible is the account of the coming of the Holy Spirit on the Apostles. I am remembering those tongues of fire which came down on the heads of the Apostles, when they were in the Upper Room. This happened after Our Lord had ascended into heaven. I was looking at the fire in this draughty house and suddenly there was a gust of wind and some of the flames of the fire seemed to divide into two or even three. You remember, don't you, how a great gust of wind accompanied the tongues of fire which settled on the heads of the Apostles? The gust of wind was a symbol of the presence of the Holy Spirit, and so were the tongues of fire. The tongues of fire gave out light and warmth. It is the role of the Holy Spirit to give light to the mind and warmth to our hearts. So when we receive the Holy Spirit at baptism or confirmation, it is to help us to understand the things of God better and to love him more. We also receive a kind of spiritual energy which makes us want to serve God and our neighbour, and to do so. It is grace working within us.

The other two were getting impatient and wanted to get on with the game. So I had to bring my meditation about the warm and friendly love of God to an end. We decided to move away from the fire. Having been very warm sitting in front of it, I, for my part, began to feel rather cold. That happens when we walk away from the love which we know God has for us. That is like walking into the cold – and may, also, be going out into the darkness, unless the landing light is on. Cold and darkness are symbols of the absence of God. It is sad, and rather frightening, when people are happy to be out in the cold and live in the darkness without God.

Anyone who has wandered away from God should think of coming back into the warmth, that is into the love He offers. There is warmth awaiting us all.

# The Cupboard

Under one of the staircases in this old house was a cupboard. Like many cupboards under stairs that I have known, the light bulb had gone. The brooms were stacked higgledy-piggledy and what spare space there was seemed to be occupied by the kinds of things one wanted to hide from possible visitors.

There was not much room for hiding, but as it was my turn I decided that I would get into the cupboard. As I was getting in I met Simon's father, Peter. I asked him to sit by the door and remain there, thinking that this would convey to those seeking me that he knew that there was nobody in the cupboard. I also asked him to leave the cupboard door open; there was too little air for one person, let alone for two.

I waited some time, sitting in the dark, but the dust was so thick in that cupboard that I let out an enormous sneeze. Kate happened to be passing that way so my whereabouts were now known to anybody within the distance of an ear-splitting sneeze. Kate came into the cupboard. She sat at one end, rather uncomfortably, on the golf clubs, and I sat at the other end on the only bit of spare floor that I could find. We certainly were not going to speak with each other for that would reveal to Barney where we were. We could not see each other, because the light bulb had gone. But I knew that she was there and

she knew that I was. I am very fond of Kate and have a very great respect for her. I would never wish to harm her in any way or do anything to frighten or upset her. I think she is quite fond of me. So, as we sat at opposite ends of the cupboard in total silence, Peter kept guard, as it were. I began to reflect.

Sometimes in prayer, after perhaps many weeks and months following a disciplined routine of praying each day, there may come a moment when we just know that we are in the presence of God. We cannot see Him, we cannot hear His voice. It is like sitting in the dark with a person of whom you are fond and there is no contact of any kind between the two of you. Something else links us. It is called love. I mean a love that is giving, pure and beautiful. At such moments we just know that we are in the presence of God, that He is loving us and as a result of that we want to love Him in return. I do not know how often this happens to people in prayer. It may be quite frequent but, on the other hand, it may be once in many years. It comes generally within the context of our daily effort to raise our minds and hearts up to God.

The sense of the presence of God includes a conviction that one day we shall see Him as He is. In that vision, we shall find that happiness for which we were made, and which eludes us in this world. It is something to which we look forward. It is an experience too deep for words to express or even thoughts to contain. I have learned this from those specially gifted by God. I may have misunderstood how it works or what the mystics say. Suffice to conclude that we may admire what these persons report, and recognise that there are different gifts in the Church. If ours is a lesser one, then do not fret. We wait upon God to give us those gifts which He considers necessary both for us and His Church.

With Peter sitting at the door and total silence within the cupboard poor Barney was quite unable to find us. So I had a wonderful opportunity to continue with my meditation. I just reflected quietly that the love that I knew Kate had for me was just a reflection of a greater love which God has for each one of us. I have often reflected that human love is the instrument we can use to explore the meaning of the word 'love' in God. I just went on living with that thought but then, alas, my meditation was cut short as I sneezed once more – thanks to the dust – and Barney leapt in and that round was over.

# *The Kitchen*

The kitchen seemed an unsatisfactory place in which to hide. The larder looked to be the most promising place. But Barney had already hidden there. We didn't like using the same place twice. It showed a lack of imagination, quite apart from other unwritten rules of the game. Anyway, the only possible place other than the larder, was between the deep-freezer and the fridge. There was not much room. Kate's attempt to squeeze in between was not too successful. That is why I found her so easily. I just sat in a chair in the kitchen as we both waited for Barney to find us. The washing machine was on. I was fascinated just watching as if it were a television set. Of course the intellectual content of that viewing was negligible. I counted the number of times my scarlet pyjamas seemed to appear. Quite often. But that should not have been part of my meditation. I had to stop being mesmerised by the washing machine. My eyes wandered to the dishwasher. I was surprised to find such a modern device in so ancient a house. Oh dear, that, too, did not seem quite relevant to prayer. Of course, it was less distracting than the washing machine. It made funny gurgling noises, which were a bit distracting. Nonetheless I started to reflect.

My first thought was to regret the inventing of a dishwasher.

Washing up together used to be a good community exercise. Barriers were broken down. We were all at one in the great enterprise of washing up the supper things and, generally, the breakfast dishes too. But it was more tactful not to notice that. Good gracious, I am showing off! How often, I said to myself, do I wash up? Very rarely, I must confess. So stop talking about it as if you were an expert, I said to myself. In any case if you had to wash up every day you would soon be clamouring for a dishwasher. Yes, I suppose so.

## The Kitchen

If I had to wash up every day, cook, and tidy the kitchen, I would not be able to pray. I wouldn't have time. Maybe in the evening I would be able to slip away on my own just to pray. So would I only be pleasing to God when I prayed? Would He be quite uninterested in the washing up, the cooking, the tidying up?

He is interested in all these activities, and very much so. After all we learn in the Book of Genesis that we had to till the soil, cultivate the land, use our God-given gifts to draw out of the created universe all its latent potential. Work, we are told, in that same book, is natural to us. Part of being human is to be able to work. The fact that it is accompanied 'by the sweat of our brows' is a consequence of sin. Work is good. God rejoices to see us at work and developing His creation. No task is too menial or unimportant for Him. Everything counts in His eyes unless spoilt by sin.

There is another reason why all work is pleasing to God. Our Lord spent thirty years of His life living the life of an ordinary person in Nazareth. So much so that when He began to preach people were amazed. Surely, they said, this is the son of Joseph. We know Him. Our Lord worked. There must have been washing up and cooking in the Holy Family's home at Nazareth. Those thirty years of Our Lord's hidden life emphasised an important point. Ordinary daily living is our way of serving God. Everything we do, except for sin, can be and should be an act of love. It brings us back to considering the sacrament of the present moment. At any one time, whatever we are doing or wherever we are, we can send a quick prayer to our Father in heaven. His will is made known to us through the duties we are called upon to carry out at any given time. Doing His will and accepting it is part of growing holy. There are hundreds, indeed thousands, of people who have worked quietly and unnoticed over the years, and have become saints that way. They may not be formally canonised. We keep their feast on 1st November every year.

When we work – at whatever trade or function – God the Father is, so to speak, reminded of His Son doing likewise. In fact the reality is even more wonderful. Because we are baptised God the Father recognises in each one of us a family likeness. We have been christened, to use an ancient English term, and that means we are made like Christ. We no longer live, but Christ lives in us when we are in grace. Rejoice, then, when you go about your work. The heavens could open. You might hear a voice calling out 'this is my beloved son, my beloved daughter, in him, in her I am well pleased'. Don't drop the dish you are holding if you hear such a voice. If in fact you do slip away from time to time, just to be alone with God in prayer, then with the ears of faith you will hear that voice saying: 'I am pleased with you; I like what you are doing; enjoy it and do it well.'

You and I tend to make Sunday different from every other day. From one point of view that is right. It should be different, for it should be a day with prayer playing a major part (for example, attendance at Mass) and a day of rest. It should be a day for the family and to share with friends. Does that seem out of date? Why not share Sunday lunch and enjoy being with others? Oh dear, it does sound dated. Sad.

I wonder how many more times my pyjamas are destined to hurtle round the washing machine. Will they shrink? Maybe next time I'll wash them myself. I have done shirts, so why not pyjamas? If I do I'll try to make the washing an act of love of God. I shall try to do that ordinary chore for the honour and glory of God, as Christ did. Far-fetched? Not at all, just common sense. If everyday work is not part of His plan for us, then work would lose its ultimate significance and importance.

We sanctify our work by offering it up to God. The gifts brought up to the altar at Mass represent us and our work, 'fruit of the earth and work of human hands', we pray at Mass. Those gifts are offered by Christ Himself.

# *An Interlude*

I have to admit that I was beginning to find this game of hide-and-seek a little tedious. I know that this is wrong but at my age it was not easy to keep up with the enthusiasm of the two children, with whom I was playing.

Why, I said to myself, I must look after my own health! So I made myself comfortable in front of the television, leaving Kate and Barney to get on with the game. I turned on the television set. There appeared a picture of a long line of men, women and children, tired and hungry, fleeing from one country to another. It was a terrible sight.

I began to think. Was this tragedy any concern of mine? And if it were, what should I do? Send a few pounds to an aid agency? Yes, that certainly. But was that all? Then a voice within me said: 'It is no business of yours' and went on – in Latin surprisingly – 'Num sim custos fratris mei?' ('Am I my brother's keeper?'). Am I?

Many would say, I reflected, that I had no responsibility as a bishop. 'Concern yourself with helping people to save their souls. Religion is a private and personal matter. Leave social matters to others, social workers and politicians. Stick to teaching people the faith (which you are bad at) and how to say prayers (which you don't really do).' Of course, I must teach the truths of the faith. I must prepare people for the next world. I must speak about the spiritual life and about prayer. But is that all?

As I was discussing all this with myself, I thought I saw a gentleman sitting next to me. Truth to tell, I had dozed off to sleep. The gentleman was present in my dream. I asked him his name. He said, 'I am called Dives'. 'What have you got to say to me?' I asked. 'Don't make the mistake I made,' he said. 'I was living comfortably, concerned only for my own welfare. Now I have to watch the poor man, Lazarus, being so happy while I am quite miserable. I have to suffer for my neglect of people like him.' 'What should you have done?' I asked. 'Well,' Dives responded, 'get your New Testament out and read chapter 25 of St Matthew's Gospel. If you feed the hungry, shelter the homeless, then you do it to Christ Himself. If you do not, then you fail Him. If you want any further confirmation of how to respond to the command to love your neighbour, then read the story about the Good Samaritan.' I woke up. Dives had gone. That was a relief. He made me feel very uncomfortable. And he looked and sounded so miserable.

Now awake, I tried to sort out my thoughts. Of course, it is important to help people in need. I shall send them money, give them clothes and blankets. Is that all? I then remembered the Catholic Church's social teaching, and especially all that has been written by Popes these last hundred years. The foundation of that teaching is the dignity of the human person. In virtue simply of our common humanity, we must surely respect and honour one another. Each individual has a value which can never be lost and must never be ignored. We are each made in the image and likeness of God; each one precious in His eyes; each person matters. We are members of one human family; we need one another, we are dependent on one another. This interdependence is called solidarity. Yes, I should weep for the misery of another. I shall send a cheque off tomorrow. Is that all?

Once I had decided to send the cheque, and therefore done all that I believed I could do, I casually picked up an old copy of *The Times* to while away the time. The sports page first attracted my attention. Important events had been unfolding in the city of my birth. Then I glanced at the front page. I was struck by the smiling face of a thirteen-year-old girl called Sandra. She looked as lovely as her companion sitting next to her. Sandra had lost a leg. She was one of some 70,000 people who had been victims of the 12 million mines lurking under-ground awaiting their next victim. Sandra would have been no more than another statistic had she not made the front page of *The Times*. She might have been your daughter, or my sister. She is one of us. She hurts in the same way as we hurt. She laughs and she cries as every human does. Sandra is my concern, simply because she is human like me.

I went on thinking about these things. I said to myself, 'No – sending a cheque is not enough'. I, like others, have to do what I can to understand, and then help, remove the causes of poverty and misery. It is one thing to treat the symptoms, another to get rid of the illness. I shall, then, continue to be concerned about life issues, homelessness, unemployment, poverty, and say so. And I shall be concerned, too, about fair trading arrangements, or the lack of them, which affect developing countries. I shall do what I can to have something done about international debt when it affects Third World countries adversely, about banning landmines, about the exploitation of people or the environment.

Loving our neighbour as ourselves must involve us in trying to do something practical to have things changed when indeed change is demanded. When it comes to reforming unjust structures, those who exercise power, politicians and experts, have a special responsibility. They, surely, must be concerned for the common good – that sum of those social conditions which makes it possible for individuals to realise their human potential. Religion is always personal, but it is never private.

My reflection continues: 'No, I won't get caught up as a bishop with the party political process; I won't always pretend to know the best policies to adopt to achieve the common good. I don't. It is not my job as a cleric to do so. But I cannot fail to be concerned for the welfare of every person. I should urge others with the responsibility to take appropriate action in the interests of the common good, having regard especially to the weakest and most vulnerable members of society.'

We are not all in a position to relieve the misery of our neighbours, especially when they are in a far distant land. Those who are, should. For the rest of us it is partly a question of creating an attitude throughout our society, that when others are suffering or wherever human dignity is threatened or violated, then action should be taken. But it also requires us to act as individuals, in groups or voluntary associations to help meet those human needs we come across. The Gospel demands it; our common humanity cries out for it. Common sense dictates it.

I was reluctant to tear myself away from that armchair. It was very comfortable, and so was I. Oh dear. How I wish I were less preoccupied with my own welfare, and more with that of others! It is never too late to start. I don't want to join Dives or be like him. I will think more about Lazarus, especially when he is homeless, or has just left prison with nowhere to go, or if he has trodden on a landmine. I shall see what I should do.

# The Fog

I did something which I think was probably wrong. Now there is an unwritten convention among hide-and-seek players that you do not in fact go back again to the place where you have already hidden. But I thought if I did this, then I might get quite a bit of peace. I also hoped the two children would forgive my decision to go back behind the curtain where before I had been able to sit comfortably. It was now unlikely that I would be found by them. I now had a chance to continue with my prayers.

As I looked out of the window I noticed that the fog was

still as thick as ever. The last time I hid there, it suddenly lifted and I saw the garden. I was able to reflect then on how sometimes the fog, which seems to separate us from God, lifts a little and we see something which reminds us of God. The beauty of the garden spoke to me of the beauty which is in God. This time the fog suggested quite another train of thought. Quite often people who are leading good lives, doing their best to pray well and serve God, can and do go through very dark periods. They feel lost. The fog around them appears to become thicker and thicker. They can see nothing clearly. They are in turmoil or just empty. They have no peace within. They want somebody to come and help them. The light has gone out of their minds. They experience no warmth in their hearts. They may rush from one spiritual book to another to find a solution, or go in search of a spiritual director, but in vain.

There is another way of reacting. A sheep which has wandered away from the rest of the flock gets itself caught up in a whole heap of briars. The more it struggles to get free, the more it becomes entangled. As it struggles, a great fog comes down and hides the surroundings from the sheep's eyes. The sheep is lost, lonely and unhappy. It has exhausted itself struggling to get free. Then through the fog it hears the sound of the shepherd's voice. It does not see him, but knows that he is coming in search of it. The shepherd approaches, disentangles the sheep from the briars and sets it free. Indeed more than this, the shepherd carries the sheep on his shoulder back to a place where there is no fog and cold but only light and warmth.

## The Fog

For many of us who believe that we are doing our best to pray and respond to God's will this kind of situation will occur. It happens, I believe, so that we may recognise our need to be helped by another. We have to learn patience. We must wait. We may have to wait a long time, entangled by our problems and unable to see where to go. When Our Lord called Himself the Good Shepherd and then told us the story about the lost sheep, we learn something which is not only very helpful but profoundly important. I often feel like a lost sheep surrounded by fog, but I am happy to remain so, waiting for the Good Shepherd to come and find me. He delights in my patience, and in my trusting of Him that indeed He will come. I may read many books seeking a way out of my problems; I may search out wise and experienced spiritual guides, and find no solutions. True, God may speak to us through a book or a person. Sometimes He leaves us to wait, alone and confused. It is a purifying process, as we come to rely less – or if at all – on our own resources, and have to abandon ourselves into God's hands. 'Into thy hands, Lord, I commend my spirit.' Christ prayed these words on the Cross. They are good friends for us when our need is desperate.

With that lovely thought in mind I just sat behind those musty curtains and prayed, 'Lord, please keep looking for me, I am waiting to be found.'

# The Medicine Chest

We were running out of places to hide. I suppose that the other two would regard the bathroom to be out of bounds. Well, maybe. But I chose it anyway. I got bored waiting to be found. The only interesting thing in a bathroom is the medicine chest. I opened its door. I then thought better of it. A medicine chest is a bit private. Why should everyone know what is wrong with me? I closed the door and wondered how to start my prayer.

It is not usual to start reflecting on a medicine chest. We cannot blame them, I suppose, because they were not invented or designed to provide inspiration for prayer. They have a limited function. Well, that sounds a bit dismissive. I can almost hear this one grumbling: 'Where do you go when you have a headache? Why, you rush to me to get the wonder pill that will bring comfort to your head.' No, I must be grateful for the medicine chest, and for all the half-empty bottles and unused lozenges, bought in a mini-state of panic at the chemist down the road. 'Think about me for a moment,' I thought I heard the medicine chest say. 'I have a message for you.' So I began to think.

Yes, you do remind me of an important aspect of life. Not for me great pain and suffering. I admit that I am not like Mrs

C. down the road who has been in a wheelchair for the last thirty years. Nor was I born with some disability that makes walking difficult and running impossible. I just have the common cold from time to time, an ache here and a pain there. Oh dear, and I do let everyone know about it. 'You do whinge', someone told me recently. He was right. I do.

I have seen great courage and cheerfulness in persons I have visited in hospital. I have admired the sick with whom I have been to Lourdes. They have, by their patience and goodness, preached sermons as effective as any I have heard. 'Yes,' I have said to myself, 'that is the way to be.' What is their secret? They have learned to embrace God's will. Then an old question comes to mind. Why should God choose some to suffer so, and maybe for a whole lifetime? God's ways are not ours. We never know what His real plan is. There is much that we do not understand.

So what about the sermon preached by the sick and infirm? They have, I believe, a special vocation. It is to show in their lives the pain and suffering of Christ. They share in his passion. St Paul once wrote that we have to make up in our lives what is still wanting in the sufferings of Christ. I never did understand what that meant, well, not exactly. I know that it says something very important nonetheless. Christ's suffering was necessary for us. Again we touch on something here we cannot fully understand. His passion was part of His redeeming work. Furthermore, He asks some of us to join Him in that work, some more closely than others, all of us at some time or other.

There is another thought to bear in mind: by sharing in our

suffering and pain, Christ has sanctified them and made them of value to us. Our task is to learn how to accept the minor health problems of every day. It isn't easy to learn to thank God for that pain in the foot (no, it wasn't gout) or for that sore throat that made talking so difficult. I have never really accepted to have to remain in bed when there was something important that I was supposed to do. I must learn, Lord, to accept the minor health problems and to thank you for them. When the big problems come, I shall be ready, or at least less unprepared.

In quiet moments, when reflecting on suffering and pain, I think it a bit 'over the top' to identify my minor aches and pains with the passion of Christ. Then I remind myself that nothing is too small or insignificant in the eyes of God. Mine may be a very light cross to carry, but it is still the Cross, and happily I know that Christ comes to help me carry it as once Simon of Cyrene helped Him.

Yes, Lord, I admire the chronically sick, those who have been incapacitated all their lives, those who have grown through suffering and avoided resentment or bitterness. I let my thoughts run on and I asked God to help me not to 'whinge', to embrace suffering when it comes and to rejoice even if, and when, I am visited by great suffering. That last bit was hard to pray about, but I did my best to be sincere. I prayed especially for help to see with the eyes of faith the value for me and others of the pain and suffering that may come to me. So my prayer continued. . . . It was suddenly interrupted by a loud scream. It was Barney. I rushed to the door of the bathroom and shouted, 'What's wrong, Barney?' He came along in tears with a grazed knee. It wasn't too serious. But he cried. I said: 'For heaven's sake, Barney, stop crying.' I wanted to say to him: 'Our Lord suffered, you know, why can't you?' But he is too young to understand that. Not for the first time in my life I knew I was being a hypocrite. I haven't understood that either!

# *Death*

Barney was really being very tiresome about that grazed knee. I tried to find a plaster for it in the medicine chest but there was none the right size. There never is. So off he went to find his mother. That meant that our game couldn't go on for the present. That suited me. I could go on trying to meditate. I decided that I might as well stay where I was – in the bathroom.

I had already reflected on sickness. I had tried to understand how the small but irritating aches and pains could be very much part of my spiritual life. Earlier on in my reflections I had done all I could to keep my thoughts off death. It never quite works to do so, especially when we know we have more years behind us than ahead of us.

First thoughts about death are normally ones of fear and dread. It is partly having to face the unknown, partly the recoiling from the final agony, as we lie helpless and perhaps wired up to all those machines competing for access to our body. On a bad day there is that common fear which tells us that there is no future, only a blank, nothing. We are no more. And then another thought comes to trouble us, and it is how quickly we are forgotten. We may not be worth a biography, just a short notice in a Catholic paper, if that. Yes, soon forgotten, save perhaps to linger in the memory of one who did love us, and will miss us every day. Some do not even have that. Then in a very bad moment I think about the relief my demise will bring to some people. I do worry about the insensitive and clumsy ways I have handled some people, about my selfishness... no, I won't go on listing my faults here. It is a bit embarrassing. 'Don't forget' – I once heard a great Abbot say – 'when you die somebody will be relieved'.

How much more gloomy can these reflections about death become? Maybe there is an instinctive human reaction to death which fills us with horror or makes us fearful. Those thoughts can come to haunt on a sleepless night. The darkness of the night matches the darkness that is within us, when depression or fear have become our masters – it should not be so.

There is pain in death, Lord, and it must be so, for death is the wages of sin. None can escape its payment. But surely Christ did not die just to share this aspect of our humanity. He died to make death a gateway to something else. He overcame death, as he atoned for its cause, sin. He rose from the dead, and he lives on now, making intercession on our behalf. So, death, where is your sting now? Faith, not reason, comes to our rescue. It is faith that enables us to turn that foe into a friend. As Christ died and rose from the dead, so shall it be in our case too. Does faith lead to self-delusion? Can it stifle the voice that says: 'There is no God, you have no future.' But there is another voice that speaks within us. It is not the voice that brings news that depresses and frightens. It has another message. 'You have loved so many persons in your life; you have longed to enjoy total fulfilment and happiness; are you to be frustrated and denied that which you have sought throughout your life?' It is not so. Faith carries you where reason cannot go. You may have desired so much, perhaps often suffered intensely, been frustrated and saddened, but none of this proves that there is a place where compensation will be given and dreams be realised. But unaided reason is rescued by faith. Some instinct, a positive and optimistic one, speaks of hope leading to life after death. In the animal world the instinct for survival is strong. It is so with humans as well. We want to go on, unless overwhelmed by depression or weariness. Our fear is that we may not. That instinct beckons us. Our mind says, 'It may be; it must be'. Then faith finally takes over, and with triumph declares, 'It is so'. Yes, there is life after death. The instinct for survival is a true one; it does not deceive. How could it be otherwise since it is God-given? Faith brings the reassurance which instinct was seeking.

The vision of God is that for which we were made. To see Him, as He is, face to face, that is the moment of ecstasy, the ever-present 'now' of total happiness.

I wandered into the ward to see him, for I heard that he was dying. I looked at him. He was wired to every machine parked about his bed. A mask covered his face. He could neither see nor hear, until in fact I spoke. I said: 'I shall be in Lourdes soon and shall pray for you.' A smile played upon his lips. He understood. Then I walked away. He seemed very much alone, abandoned by all, his only companions the machines. I thought: 'How awful, how lonely.' Then I realised that he lay alone in a sea of love, for God is everywhere and God is love.

He then floated into another world sustained by that 'love' to meet Him whose love is all that is worth having.

I now have no fear of death. I look forward to this friend leading me to a world where my parents, my brother and other relatives are, and my friends. I shall see those who fashioned me in my monastic life. I shall see Abbot Byrne, Anthony, Kenneth, David, Barnabas, Hubert, James, Denis, Robert, Peter, Walter, John and many others. I look forward to that.

# *Epilogue*

I am sure that you have guessed how this book will end. Now many of us play hide-and-seek often. We don't play with Kate and Barney, or with any other children. We play with God. It is not that He hides from us, we hide from Him. He is the one who is looking for us, trying to find us. We hide, because we may not be able to face being found. Life can be less complicated if we keep hidden from Him. We don't have to bother about Sunday Mass. There is no need to pray. We may even convince ourselves not only that He isn't looking for us, but that He doesn't exist at all! And yet He goes on searching us out. Why? Because He seeks intimacy with us.

What authority have I for saying this? God's own authority. One day the Apostle Philip said to Our Lord, 'Lord, show us the Father and we shall be satisfied' (John 14,8). I have referred to this text earlier on in this book. Reference was made to it in the Prologue when I wrote about starting points to prayer. I repeat it here because it is, in my view, a pivotal text for our exploration of what God is like. Then Jesus said to Philip, 'Have I been with you so long, and yet you do not know me, Philip? He who has seen me has seen the Father: how can you say, "Show us the Father"?' Our Lord went on to explain. 'Do you not believe that I am in the Father and the Father is in me? The words that I say to you I do not speak on my own authority . . . believe me that I am in the Father and the Father in me . . .' (John 14, 9–11).

These are words which we should ponder and about which we should pray. I make no apology for coming back to them. They are so important. Jesus in all His words, actions and attitudes reveals to us what God is like, for He is both God and man. Jesus translates into human words, attitudes and actions the thoughts of God Himself.

With this in mind, we may now go to an example from St Luke's Gospel where we can see how God goes in search of us. Read chapter 15 of that Gospel. There are three stories. We read about a shepherd in search of a lost sheep, then about a woman who turned her house upside-down to find a lost coin, and lastly about a wayward son returning to his father.

The chapter starts with a most consoling observation on the part of St Luke. 'Now the tax collectors and sinners were all drawing near to hear him. And the Pharisees and the Scribes murmured saying, "This man receives sinners and eats with them".' No excuses there for anyone tempted to protest unworthiness, and use that as a reason to hide from God.

That shepherd should never have left the ninety-nine which were safe and risk losing more of them. Surely he should have cut his losses. What he did in leaving the ninety-nine seems, on reflection, almost reckless. This tells us how persistent God is in wanting to find us. It shows us how important we are to Him. He doesn't want to lose any of us. We are precious like that coin which the woman sought with such intensity. Her coin may not have been worth much, but it was of the greatest value to her. So it is with God and us.

The story of the Prodigal Son teaches us another important point. God seeks us but does not force us. We remain free to be found or not, to return to Him or not. The father in the parable is waiting for his son to return. One day he sees him coming home. 'While he was yet at a distance' (v.20), the father, we are told, 'had compassion, and ran and embraced him and kissed him'. That verse 20 has taught me, more than any other passage in the Bible, what God is like. Read it again and again, let your mind dwell on it. Ask the Holy Spirit to cast His light upon it. Your heart will then begin to warm. When that happens you have been found, and you will not have any desire to hide again.

There often follows another and different experience. God seems to have hidden from you. You find yourself wondering: Why? Have I displeased Him? You ask, Am I in sin? Have I been neglectful of Him? Maybe. But you will probably be able to say that you have done nothing to displease Him, nor are you conscious of any deliberate serious sin. So what has happened? Once He has found you, it will be His turn to hide. He wants you to go in search of Him all over again, as if you had not already found Him. The lover, God, wants you, the beloved, to go looking for Him. Then the roles are reversed. The seeker, you, becomes the one who is sought. Hide-and-seek is a game for lovers, not just for children. It is also a game for God and for you. Sometimes you will be the seeker, at other times the one that is sought.

He will, I think, whisper into your ear words from the

seventeenth-century philosopher Pascal: 'Be consoled, you could not be seeking me if you had not found me already.' Yes, He says to you: 'I want you, of course I do, and I know you want me. Go in search of me and you will certainly find me.'